living in the future

GEOFFREY HOYLE

living in the future

illustrated by Alasdair Anderson

Finding-Out Books

Parents' Magazine Press
New York

Library of Congress Cataloging in Publication Data

Hoyle, Geoffrey.
  2010: living in the future.

  (Finding-out books)
  SUMMARY: Describes one idea of the streamlined,
automated world of 2010 where beds are built into
the floor, school is attended by vision phone, and
groceries and dinner are ordered and delivered by
computer.
  1. Forecasting–Juvenile literature.
2. Civilization, Modern–1950-   –Juvenile
literature. [1. Forecasting. 2. Civilization,
Modern–1950-   ] I. Anderson, Alasdair, illus.

II. Title.
CB161.H69 1974   901.95   73-12832
ISBN 0-8193-0708-4

The world we live in has changed very fast since your grandparents were children. At that time, horses and wagons did much of the work that trucks do today. There were no television sets, no air conditioners, no computers, no trips to the moon. Nobody worried about pollution, or shortage of fuel.

Some of the changes that have come about—especially in medicine—have been very good for us. Others have not been so good.

Scientists and inventors are working all the time, and no one really knows what the world will be like when you have grandchildren of your own.

But it is fun to guess what it may be like, and that is what this book is about. It is one person's idea of how people will live in the year 2010. When you have read it, you can decide whether or not you would like it that way, or what you would do to make it different.

The year is 2010.

"It is seven o'clock," says an alarm clock hidden in the wall. Suddenly the room is filled with the sound of music. Time to get up—off the floor.

In the year 2010 you do not sleep on a bed. There

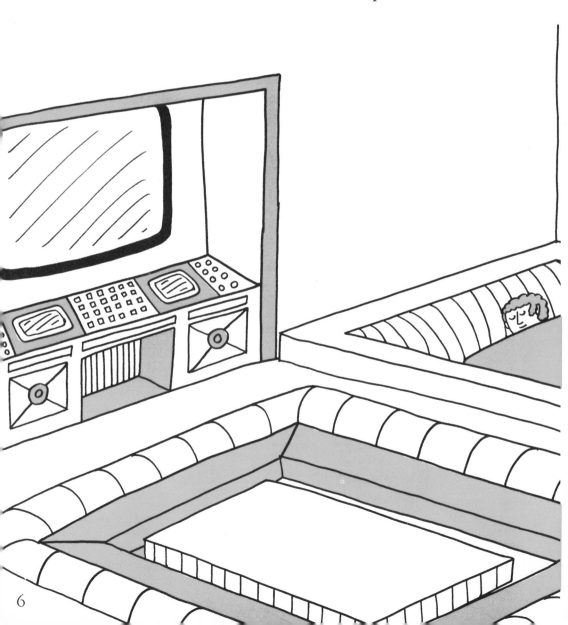

are no beds, no tables, no chairs. The floor is made for sitting, sleeping, and walking on. It is soft where you sit or sleep, hard where you need a table or desk.

Your home is very carefully planned. No family

8

lives in a house or apartment too large or too small for them. Every room has several uses. The bedroom is also an office, and the kitchen is a living room. In 2010 there must be no wasted space. There are so many people in the world that every inch of ground must be used wisely.

9

In your tiny bathroom there is no tub, just a
shower. The shower makes it very easy to keep
yourself clean. There are no faucets for hot and cold

water, no soap to slither out of your fingers, no need for towels.

You just set the dial for the water temperature

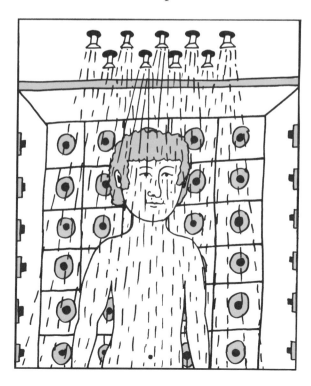

and step in. Water pours down from small jets in the ceiling.

Then foaming soap flows over you. More water

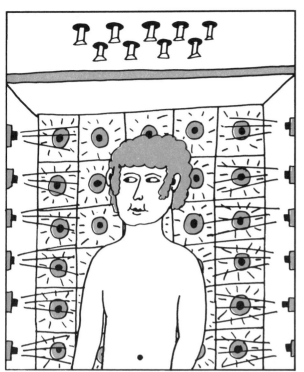

rinses you. Finally, a blast of warm air comes from
vents in the side of the shower to dry you.
Now you are ready to put your clothes on.

13

As you walk around the house, you can feel that the temperature is just right. There is a boiler that not only heats or cools the air but cleans it. Every hour, air is sucked into the boiler from

all over the house. The air passes through a filter which removes all the dust and dirt. From here it goes into a humidifier which either takes water out of the air or puts it back in. This keeps the air neither too damp nor too dry. Finally the air is heated and blown back into the house. So, without anyone lifting a finger, the house is warm and clean.

In the year 2010 everyone wears a jumpsuit and shoes. The clothes may look odd, but they are very sensible. The jumpsuits and shoes are made in thousands of colors, from a material so light you can hardly feel it. The material keeps you warm when it is cold and cool when it is hot.

Now you are up and dressed it is time to go to the kitchen for breakfast. On one wall of the kitchen there is a cooking unit, made up of small ovens, refrigerators, deep freezers, and cold-storage compartments. All the cooking is done

16

automatically. It is controlled electronically by a small built-in computer. There is a control panel to work the cooker. It looks like a typewriter, with rows of numbered and lettered keys. To order breakfast, you spell out what you want on the control panel.

BACON—WELL DONE. TWO EGGS—MEDIUM. TOAST.
TEA—MILK AND SUGAR.

After a moment's pause, the bacon appears in one
of the ovens, then the eggs. Toast pops out of the
toaster and a light shows you the tea is ready.

18

You pick up a disposable cup, plate, knife, fork, and spoon and collect your breakfast.

It is easy to see when your food is cooked by watching the lights above the ovens: RED for cooking, GREEN for ready, and YELLOW for keeping warm.

The bacon and eggs came from the cold storage to the ovens on a conveyor belt. In the oven, infra-red heat cooked them in seconds.

The tea is made from hot water, taken from a cylinder and mixed with the tea, milk, and sugar from a container.

The toast starts life as ordinary sliced bread. An arm in the toaster picks up the bread and passes it in front of heating elements. When it is toasted, the arm throws you the toast.

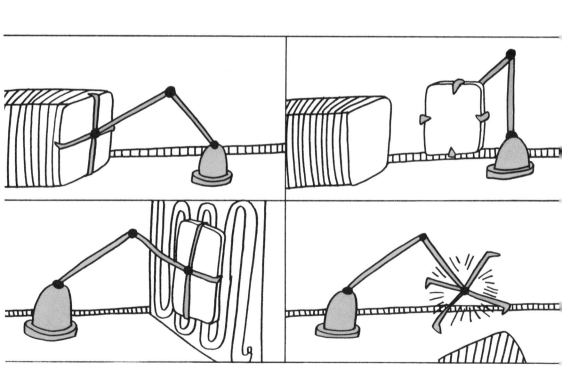

When you have finished, you take your plate, cup, knife, fork, and spoon and drop them down the waste disposer. They are ground up and washed away into the sewers.

All the food and drink are delivered right into the kitchen from the supermarket. They come in an electric truck. The delivery man opens the refrigerators, deep freezers, and cold-storage units from outside the house and places his load in the right containers.

You never need to go shopping for the weekly groceries. You just dial the supermarket on the vision phone. A list of departments and their numbers appears on the screen.

When you dial the food department, you will see

BREAD
37¢ = 1 LB.
FRUIT CAKE
$1.50 = 2 LBS.

a picture of it. The picture shows all the different foods and their prices.

You give your order over the phone and it is recorded at the supermarket by a tape recorder. Later the same day the electric delivery truck arrives with your order.

When you have bought your groceries, you must pay for them. The bill appears on the vision desk below the vision phone. It is important to check the bill because computers can make mistakes.

When you are satisfied the bill is correct, you dial your bank number. It is printed on the bill at once. You sign the bill by placing your thumb on the vision desk alongside the bank number. An

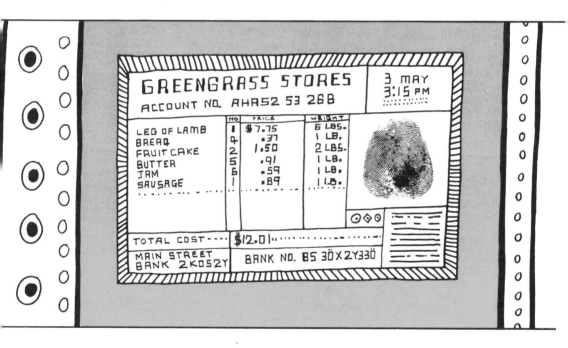

electronic thumbprint is taken and transferred onto the bill.

Signing bills in this way stops anyone else from using your bank number. No two people have the same thumbprint.

The bill is finally sent to the bank which pays the shop the money owed.

At nine o'clock it is time for school. Inside a large
closet in your bedroom there is a vision phone and
vision desk. As soon as you dial your school number,
the screen lights up, and there is your teacher.

In 2010 your home is your classroom. The teacher's classroom is in his or her home. In the teacher's room there are many vision screens connected to the vision phone. On these screens the teacher can see all the children in the class.

Opposite the screens there is a blackboard. Whatever the teacher writes on the board can be seen on the children's vision desks.

Even if you are at home by yourself, you can still talk to your friends during class time. You dial a friend's number and his face appears in a corner of your screen.

The vision phone and vision desk are electronic marvels of the twenty-first century.

The vision phone is a telephone that allows you to see the person you are talking to. He or she can see you, too.

A small camera and screen are placed in front of the phone. The camera takes the pictures and the screen shows them to you.

The vision desk is more complicated than the phone and can do different jobs. It also contains a camera and screen. The glass on top of the screen is made in a special way so that when you write on it, the camera can photograph what you write.

School work would be impossible without the vision desk. When the teacher writes a sum on the blackboard, the figures are shown on the desk.

To answer the question you take your electronic pen and start writing on the desk.

If the teacher sees that you are going wrong, he or she can correct you.

All the school work that is done on the vision desk is recorded on a giant school computer.

The computer can also be used for recording homework. Once the work is done, your teacher marks it by calling the computer.

You can always find out how well you have done by calling the computer before school begins.

To look at your past school work you dial the

school computer. It takes the computer only a few seconds to find the work.

To find what you want you use two buttons on the control panel. Press one button and the pages move forward; press the other, and the pages move backward.

While you are at school in one room, your parents may be at work in another. People who do office work do it at home. To keep in close touch with other people in their office they use the vision phone. The vision desk is connected to their firm's computer, which stores all the office files. With this close contact between everybody in the office, it is easy to work from home.

Wherever people work—in a factory or at home, or whatever else their job might be—they will work for only three days a week. The rest of the week they can do what they like. They can play football, learn a language, or train for a new job.

With few people traveling to work there are no morning or evening rush hours—no streets crowded with cars, buses, and people. Gone are the oily smells and fumes of traffic. When people travel, they go by electric car, bus, or train.

In 2010 people can live and breathe in clean, fresh surroundings, but it was not always like this.

39

At one time, late in the twentieth century, millions of people fought their way to school and work every morning. Thick fumes lay over the streets, making people cough and cry. There were just too many people trying to get into too small a space all at the same time.

Your school
classes finish every
day at one o'clock.
After lunch it is
time to meet friends

42

at the Sports and Social Center. You can travel by electric car or in a bus.

The bus services are very good and run twenty-four hours a day. You can go anywhere in the town and know there will always be a bus back. With very little traffic on the roads it is safe for children to travel by themselves.

There is no fare to pay on the bus. All public

transportation within the town is free. You have to pay only when you travel from one town to another.

The bus stops in front of a large group of buildings, surrounded by beautiful country. The

Center and grounds are so big it would take weeks to walk around them.

Every afternoon professional games are played somewhere in the grounds. You can watch football, tennis, swimming, basketball, or play games yourself with your friends.

There are also places in the grounds where you can get away from the crowds and go fishing, horseback riding, climbing, or just walking.

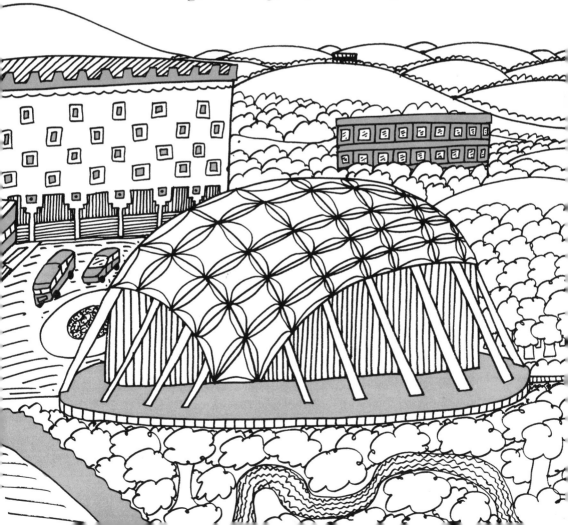

Inside, there are halls, stadiums, and swimming pools. The main stadium is so large that it can seat 500,000 people. The giant swimming pools can hold

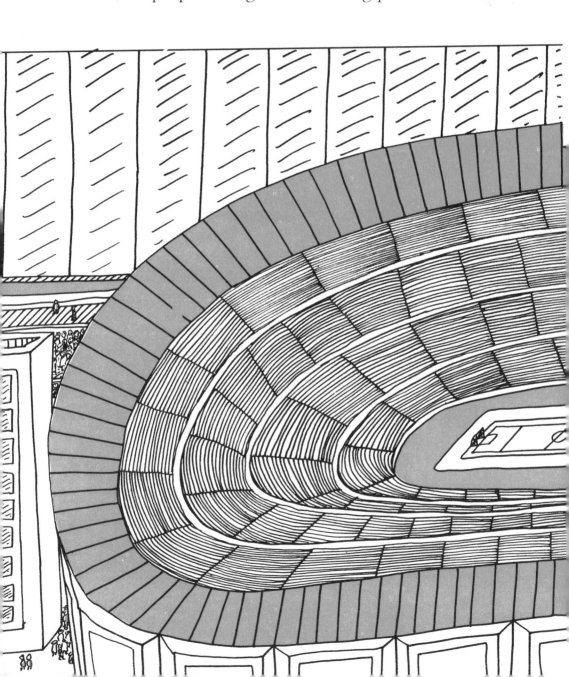

4,000 people all swimming at the same time and still have room for more.

If you walked around the Center you would wear your shoes out. So all traveling inside the building is done with elevators, moving stairs, and whole moving floors. Some of these are one-way, so it is

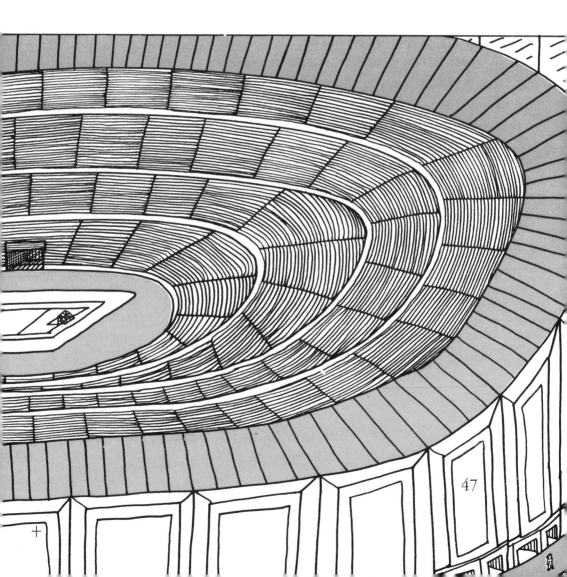

important to remember which way you want to go.

The halls and rooms on the upper floors are for hobbies. Here people make pottery, draw and paint pictures, build model airplanes, or play musical instruments. There are teachers to help you with every hobby.

A very popular room is the library. There are no books. The floor is shaped into tables and benches. Built into these tables are hundreds of vision phones. The books, films, and newspapers are all stored in the library computer.

First you dial the library index. This file contains all the books that have ever been written. It does not matter whether they were first written in Chinese or French. They will be here, translated into English. There is also an index of films and newspapers. You could spend all day watching comics, but it wouldn't be a good idea.

To select the book you wish to read, you dial the book's number. The first page appears on your screen. You can turn the pages backward or forward by using buttons on the vision phone.

If you are halfway through a book and you have to leave, there is no reason why you can't finish it when you get home. You can dial the library and the book number from home and go on with your reading.

While you are in the library, you might look at some travel film, to help you decide where to go for your summer vacation.

How about Australia? It seems a long way away, but it doesn't take so long by airplane. You will find sandy beaches, blue skies, and endless sunshine along the Great Barrier Reef.

There are glass-bottomed boats through which you could watch the tropical fish.

Or you could go to Africa, and see all the wild game roaming around the national parks.

It is very easy and cheap to travel by air. The airplanes are very small and very fast. They seat thirty people and fly them through the sky at over 4,000 miles per hour.

Seats are not reserved in advance. You just climb aboard. It is just like the town bus service.

As the afternoon draws to a close, you might like to meet your family for dinner before you go home.

A large restaurant on the roof of the Sports and Social Center covers the roof and looks more like a garden than a restaurant.

It is sometimes hard to find people in this big area. So, to help you, there is a map at the entrance with all the sitting places marked on it. Look carefully and you can see where your family have marked their place.

At the table it is easy to order. You type what you want on the control panel fixed to the table. A few minutes later the tray comes along the conveyor belt close to the table. You can see that it is your tray because there is a flag stuck to it with your table number on it.

It is interesting to see how the food arrives in the giant kitchen. The kitchen is at the far end of the roof. Like the kitchen at home, it works by computer.

55

The restaurant kitchen serves thousands of people every day. It would take hundreds of deliveries by electric trucks to keep the refrigerators and deep

freezers of the kitchen full. So the supplies are piped to it each day.

Whatever is needed in the restaurant is packed in special wrappers at a depot in the town. Everything is then placed in the pipe, which is filled with a special liquid, and pumped to the restaurant on the roof. The liquid allows packages of different weights to float. Otherwise small packages would float while large packages would sink and bang against the bottom of the pipe. When the packages reach the restaurant they are taken from the pipe, unwrapped, and put into the right containers.

The food is cooked the same way as it is at home, and sent along the conveyor belts to the customers.

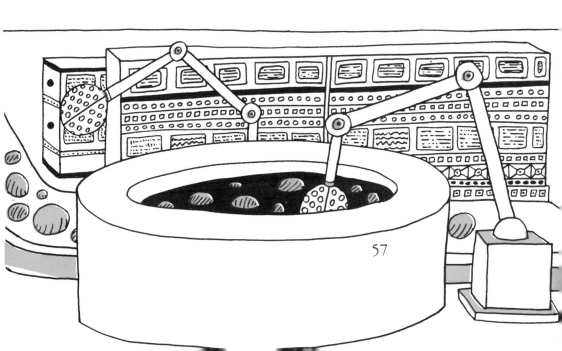

57

At the town depot there are also other pipes—
giant pipes that run the length and breadth of the
country. This is a clean, efficient way to ship
anything from a box of nails to a crane.

If someone buys a new electric car, this is the way

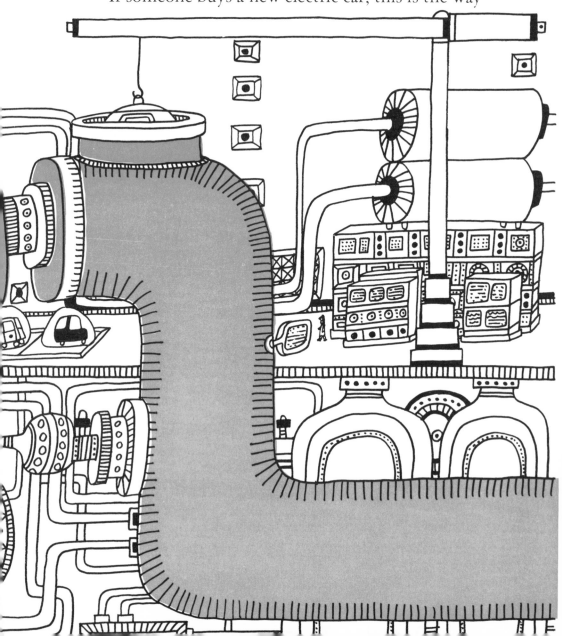

it is delivered. The car is wrapped at the factory and dropped into the pipe full of liquid. Large pumps along the pipe keep the liquid flowing. Detectors at the pumping stations make sure there are no blockages and that the goods arrive at the right place.

When the car reaches the town's main depot, it is lifted from the pipe, unwrapped, and delivered.

This is a very fast way of shipping goods. If you buy a car in the morning it will be delivered the same day.

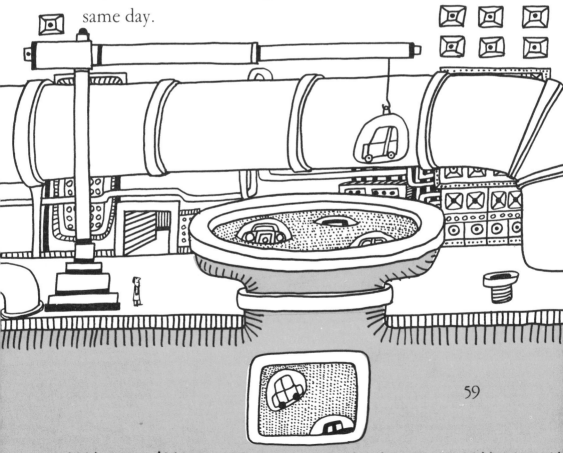

It is good to arrive home after a busy afternoon,
to relax and share your adventures with your family,
practice your guitar, or read a book.

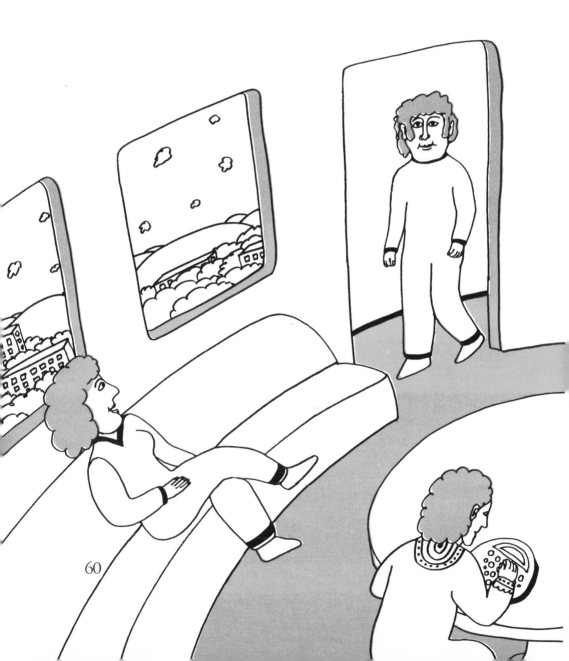

However different the world is in the year 2010,
some things will stay just the same as they are today.

Index

Africa, 52
air, travel by, 53
alarm clock, 6
amusements, 37, 45–47
apartments, planning of, 7, 9
Australia, 50
automobiles, *see* car, electric

bacon, 18, 20
bathroom, 10–13
bedroom, 9
bills, paying of, 26–27
blackboard, 29, 32
books, *see* library
breakfast, 16–19
bus, travel by, 39, 43–44

car, electric, travel by, 39,
    43;
    shipping and delivery of, 58–59
changes, 5, 61
classrooms, 29
clothes, 15
cold storage, 20
computers, 17, 26, 32, 34, 35,
    36, 55
conveyor belts, 20, 55
cooking, 16–20, 57
cooling, of homes, 14–15
cutlery, 19

deliveries, 23, 25;
    see also shipping
dishes, 19

eggs, 18, 20

food, 18-23
furniture, 7

games, professional, 45

heating, of homes, 14–15
homework, 34
houses, planning of, 7, 9

kitchen, 9, 16–17

leisure activities, 37, 45–47, 60
library, 48–50
living room, 9

music, 6

office, 9
ovens, 16, 18, 19

pipes, for deliveries, 57,
    58–59
phone, *see* vision phone
pollution, 39-40
population, 9

reading, *see* library
restaurant, in Sports Center,
    54-57

school, 28-35;
    hours of, 28, 42
shipping, 23, 25, 57-59
shopping, how done, 24-25
showering, 10-13
Sports and Social Center, 43–
    48, 54
supermarket, 23, 24

tea, 20
teachers, 28, 29, 32
telephoning, 30;
    see also vision phone
temperature. of homes, 14–15
thumbprints, 27
toast, 21
train, travel by, 39
travel, ways of, 38–39, 43–44;
    inside Sports Center, 47;
    by air, 52–53

vision desk, 26, 28, 29, 30,
    32, 36
vision phone, 24, 26, 28, 29,
    30, 32, 36
vision screens, 29

waste disposal, 22
work, places of, 36–37;
    time of, 37